Preface: Why I've Written This Book

If you think this book is going to make you immediately richer, you are sorely mistaken. What it WILL do is provide you with the strategies and information that you need in order to make your home less of an energy sink, and eventually into an energy source. I believe the transition to renewables is SO important, but it is not happening fast enough. I'm scared that the only people trying to make the transition seem fiscally responsible are solar salesmen, and the companies they work for.

My objective is to, by the end of this book, have you the homeowner realize that there are so many ways you can save money on your bills rather than immediately installing solar panels (PV panels and solar panels are synonymous throughout this book). Nobody wants to drop $20,000-$60,000 on technology they don't fully understand, and most often do not even own.

Our world is facing approximately 10 major crises. Due to my former education, receiving a B.S. in Physics with a focus in Chemical Physics, along with all but 6 credits of an M.S. level education in Sustainable Energy Systems, I have chosen to focus on climate change and the energy sectors effects on it. IF you are willing to heed my advice and make some small changes to your lifestyle, you can help me in my mission to keep our planet healthy, and the beings on it alive for as long as possible.

What makes my plan beneficial to you is that you'll wind up making your home more valuable while you do it. I want to be the man who finally introduces realistic energy solutions to every single person who can. Oh, and it won't take one dollar out of your pocket.

"We are a pebble in the river of always, the river known as infinity, the river headed towards eternity. If we wash up on the shore, our pursuit to be king, ceases"

Chapter 1: The Reason Nobody Is Telling You About This

One of my most valuable mentors once said to me, "Saving the world is a noble pursuit, but nobody is going to give a shit if you can't make them money." Up to this point, nobody has developed the ideas and structured them the way that I have because the realms of Finance and Green Living couldn't be farther apart from an educational standpoint. Me providing you with this information goes against both the renewable energy market and basic entrepreneurial tendencies. I could tell you to buy solar and how useful it is and all of that, help the solar salesmen get their money, collect stipends of my own and it would work just fine. Except you would have to buy an exorbitant amount of PV panels. I could also use my understanding of personal finance and the science behind these technologies to start a business and sell my ideas directly for profit. I don't want that. I just want the information to get out there, for as little as possible, so that change starts happening.

This is a BEHAVIORAL book, not a finance, or renewable energy book. The objective is to get you to take small actions that will not drastically affect the comforts to which you are accustomed, and to see how far those changes can really get you. Honestly, the book barely has anything to do with Green Living or Sustainability, rather, it is about accountability, discipline, and learning how to use your money effectively. The sustainable component of things just happens, as you make the changes I will discuss this later in the book.

I understand that most people want to buy something, or sell something, and suddenly, their lives are drastically improved. I'm sorry, but that isn't how this goes. YOU must change YOUR behaviors. That's the only way that using my method can work without you having to spend a single meaningful dollar. You can skip that phase and just buy the things I'll suggest later if you'd like, but according to my research, people like things way more, and are more willing to follow through, when it costs them nothing.

The biggest problem going on currently is the solar companies and their stranglehold on people who simply do not know better. Rather than telling people to bide their time, make some changes, THEN get solar panels, the companies suggest buying a monster system right off the bat. They convince people that if they buy a big enough system, they can eliminate their electric bill. I would like you to note this; even if you get nothing else out of this book. To buy an entire homes worth of electricity in solar energy before the home has been properly retrofitted is nearly impossible, at least for regular citizens like you and me.

Chapter 2: What's Wrong With Buying Solar Prematurely

I know all too well that using solar energy is crucial to the transition from fossil fuels. This is one of the most prominent selling points for the product. What this entire book explains is that there is a time and place to get your own panels.

It doesn't matter if your neighbors have them, or if you can get them with no money down (this is most likely a leasing scam) or if you really do care about the environment and want to make an impact now. The only reason to get solar panels is that your home is finally ready. Allow me to elaborate.

Solar systems, especially those made for residential use, were never meant to cover 100% of anyone's electric bill. They were designed to produce only 20% of what the average energy consumer's electric bill. This means you should drop your energy use by at least 50%, preferably 80%, before you consider buying any sort of panels.

Why don't solar salesmen tell you this? BECAUSE THEY WANT TO MAKE MORE MONEY! Any reasonable salesman is going to try and put the biggest, most expensive version of whatever they sell in front of you. It's their job, and they cannot be faulted for it. I am here to give you the consumer the knowledge to combat the status quo of solar panels and set you up to only buy the system you need, when you can afford it.

Affording something like solar panels seem easy. Especially when they tell you that they can lease you the panels for 0$ down, right? Wel , when you lease the panels, the electricity they produce is not yours. It belongs to whoever your service provider is. This is one of the biggest scams in the entire renewable energy market and people are fall ng victim to it time and time again

The basic idea behind large-scale purchases is this; when you make a purchase, you expect the item to pay for itself over a certain period, and everything after that becomes profitable to you. This is true for panels as well. You ideal y want your solar system to pay for itself in less than 20 years. That is why many warranties for such systems are good for 20-25 years, they cover the average lifespan of the system. When you lease, the chances of your system EVER paying for itself are slim at best.

Did you know that if you lease a solar system, and it underproduces, you must pay the difference back to your service provider? Having to pay out the company at the end of the year isn't very conducive to having your system pay for itself. One of the advantages of solar, which I will discuss again later, is that if your system overproduces, you get a check for the extra energy your system makes. Unfortunately, states such as Hawaii and Nevada are redacting his payout, which only increases the amount of time it will take for your panels to pay for themselves even more.

Now more than ever, the chances of leasing a solar system that will cover its own cost by the end of its life cycle are so slim, and the company you leased them from makes their money back and then some regardless. It is a sad trick that many people f nd themselves caught up in. What's worse is the salesmen normal approach is to sell everybody a system, even if the home is not a good candidate for solar.

To be an effective producer of solar power, your home needs to have a south-facing roof, no very tall trees and be in a sunny area. The chances of a system that does not fit these qualifications underproducing are so high, but that is what they count on. The big solar companies attached are essentially borrowing your roof space to put money back into their pockets, rather than into yours. Again, such is business, and they are breaking no laws, so they can't be blamed. However, this trap is avoidable.

When you buy your own panels, all the electricity they produce belongs to you. That means if they underproduce, no harm done, BUT if they overproduce you can sell your electricity back to the grid itself. Sweet deal, right? The only problem is that buying a system that will overproduce in a standard home is so insanely expensive, almost nobody can do it. If you have a massive, south-facing roof, in a sunny area, with almost no tree coverage, and an exorbitant amount of money, then by all means, just buy yourself a super system and let your panels pay for themselves over a standard 20-year period. The rest of you should continue to read.

You can always take out a loan! The bank will give it to you if you have the credit score for it, and you can just pay them back! Well then, you're paying interest on something that is already so costly. Again, the purpose is to get the panels to pay for themselves over time. As such, increasing that timeframe by taking out a $40,000 loan at a 2.5% interest rate (and this is a better case scenario) diminishes the value of the panels, and this book. With my strategy, you should be able to pay for your system out of your own pocket, if you are disciplined and patient.

Chapter 3: The Theory Behind The Plan

As stated in the previous chapter, solar panel systems are a much more reasonable purchase if your bill has been brought down significantly first. About 20% of the home's average would be ideal, but even a 50% decrease would be enough. It is ENTIRELY POSSIBLE to bring your homes electric bill down by 50% without having to use any of your hard-earned money.

In the next three chapters, I am going to suggest methods that you as a homeowner can adopt that will cost no money to make. Then as you move further through the plan, the purchases come into play. The trick to making these purchases without spending any money is using only the money that you are saving each month on the more efficient appliances and the improvements to your home.

Don't look at your saved money as simply less money that you have to spend every month, the way that most homeowners currently do. This is another way in which this is not a book about sustainability, but about BEHAVIOR. That money is more valuable than anybody seems to know. The plan, the part that everybody seems to miss (again because personal finance and energy have never been discussed as being one and the same) is to invest the money you are saving BACK INTO YOUR HOME.

The way the effects of the changes I will suggest snowball seems to be, according to my research, rather remarkable. Take your energy bills from each month of the past year. Then, follow my instructions as best you can. Take the difference between the bills and LITERALLY put the amount of money you save into an entirely separate bank account ONLY to be used for making sound residential energy reduction investments. It may start out as 2$ a month, or 20$ a month. It doesn't matter. Start putting your savings aside and watch how quickly they grow.

The most beautiful part of it all is, once you see the money growing, once you have enough saved up to make your first fiscal investment, your motivation to make the lifestyle changes will only increase. Paying less money for anything is good. When you look at it as money that you've made by putting in a little effort, it is truly an amazing feeling. You will literally be making more money off your home. Within 5-10 years of using my system, you will have drastically reduced the amount of time it will take you to pay off the investment that is your home while increasing the value of your home simultaneously. Again, any time you make a purchase, especially those made as investments, ESPECIALLY YOUR HOME, your goal should be to set that asset up to pay for itself in as little time as possible.

When you purchase a home, you take out your mortgage, put a down payment, and pay an amount every month to keep the bank off your back. But your water bill, your electric bill, your gas bill and property taxes all need to be accounted for. If you look at it this way, then your home is going to cost you much more than the interest on your mortgage loan over a 30-year period. As such, your ROI (return on investment) is greatly diminished, and for some reason, people do not realize this. If your electric bill were 0$, you could now take the money you regularly would put into your electric bill, which now costs you nothing, and throw it right at your mortgage. That's how you compound your savings. That is how you pay down your investment faster. That is the whole point of this book!

The other advantage is that the first phase is the hardest one to get through. The other phases (it consists of 3 phases) just involve making the right investments in the right order. The first phase is the one in which you really must be conscious of your energy use, and curtail your bill through your behavior, rather than new technologies. Fortunately, once you develop the proper habits and strategies, they stick with you forever, and they become easy. Some say it takes 27 days to break a bad habit or develop a good one or whatever the saying is. I think

27 days of good behavior is a piece of cake. That's less than your first month of being energy-conscious, and then according to this one theory, you've got this!

Now that I have explained the issues with the current climate in the solar industry, a little bit of the background of personal finance meeting sustainability, and that ANYONE can do this as soon as they choose, let's get into the meat of this thing.

Chapter 4: Phase 1- UNPLUG YOUR DAMNED TOASTER!

I apologize for being vulgar, but I want to drill this information into your head. Your electric is being used up in places that you wouldn't know it was without advanced knowledge of the electrical systems (i.e. your toaster) in place. All the time your appliances spend plugged in, and not in use, they are drawing 12 V of electric potential. That's constantly happening! Just unplugging your toaster when you're not using it will make you at least 15$ over the course of a year (some research shows savings as high as 100$ a year, but we'll work on the low end of things throughout the book).

Now 15$ does not seem like a lot, I understand. But the same thing is true of your coffee pot (or Keurig if that's what you're into). It's happening with every television and phone charger you've got plugged in all around the house. All the cable boxes, and the electric oven and your refrigerator(s) (my girlfriend's grandparents have 4 refrigerators in their home). I get that some of these things are inconvenient to unplug, and some cannot be unplugged. But the Keurig, toaster, microwave, and other appliances of that nature should be easy ones. At the most, they are used 5 times a day, each. Just plug them in for the 4 minutes you are running them, then take the plugs out of the outlets. It sounds like a hassle, but if you plug them into easily accessible outlets, it's a piece of cake, and in doing just those three things you are looking at an absolute minimum of 45$ extra dollars at the end of the year.

Now, the bigger stuff. Unplugging your fridge and oven isn't something you can do. Your television, cable box, gaming systems and phone chargers? Those are all doable. The problem is, they're annoying. Luckily, power strips/surge protectors exist. If you plug all your entertainment devices (or as many as you can/ are willing to, because I know restarting a cable box can be a real pain in the ass) into one surge protector, again that is easily accessible (I generally suggest hanging it on the wall behind the television so it is easy to see, and out of the reach of children) then it's just one switch to worry about. Turn it off when you're on your way out the door for work, and when you are leaving the living room to go to bed, etc. It is MUCH preferable to have one strip drawing 12 volts all the time than to have 3-6 devices all drawing 12 volts each all the time. Working under the assumption that it's 15$ a year per device, we're talking about an additional 45$ again at least. Now we're up to almost 90$ made and we haven't spent a single dollar (assuming you own power strips).

I am a person who likes to have the TV on when I'm going to bed. A curse of being a middle-class millennial I suppose. Rather than have the TV on for 8-10 hours over the course of the whole night however, I set the TV, and the Xbox one that I watch Netflix on to 2-hour inactivity timers. That way they aren't running all night, and even though they are still pulling voltage, it is an improvement.

This is one of the keynotes I want to get through with my message here. You DO NOT have to be endlessly strict with yourself and take relentless action to make sure no energy is being drawn ever.

Compromise with yourself, and your family. Do what you're willing to do, and the worst thing that happens is you grow your money to make investments with a little slower. What I've found is that when people start seeing that new bank account build up quickly, they bring it upon themselves to make a couple more changes. I could be wrong, but most people in the modern day seem to have become addicted to watching their bank accounts grow. (By the way, I suggest a credit union savings account, the 1% guaranteed interest rate is helpful once the account starts to get rather large, and it is easy to draw money from and transfer money into).

So hopefully you're using some power strips, turning off lights when you leave rooms, and unplugging your smaller scale appliances (a printer is another example) when you are not using them.

These all will make you money on your electric bill, guaranteed, and NONE of these are the biggest culprit when it comes to the cost you pay for energy. Most of the money you are spending each month on energy goes towards the heating and cooling of your home, and the heating up of your water.

Let's talk about water first, and I promise, your homes HVAC system and water heater will both come up continuously throughout this book, so PAY ATTENTION. Changing the temperature of anything takes a good deal of energy, that's just how thermodynamics works. If you could decrease how often, and by how much you needed to heat up your water, your bill will be cut drastically. I mean like, way more than making any of the changes in small appliance use will. Here's how to get started, with a few of my favorite/most straightforward methods.

Decrease the water pressure in your showers/sinks a very little bit (and I wouldn't tell your family about this one, as it seems to really tick people off when they find out there's less water pressure, even if the difference is negligible). Less pressure means less water coming out over the course of a shower/dishwashing session, and as such, less water needs to be heated up. Easy, effective, and realistically, this doesn't change your day to day life at all. Washing your clothes with cold rather than hot water (unless the clothing calls for hot water specifically) is another way to minimize the use of your water heater without spending any money. That's at least once a week where you were once heating water, and now won't be, and all the research suggests that this does not affect how clean your clothing comes out whatsoever. Reducing your water heating costs with these methods costs nothing and is a huge step in getting you a good chunk of money to start making investments with.

The final step of phase 1 is changing the amount of heating and cooling that your home requires. In the winter time it's heating of course and vice versa in the summertime. The scary part about this for most people is the sacrifice of comfort. Well, do not fear! A change in your thermostat setting of only 2-degrees (warmer in the summer, cooler in the winter) can produce great results in terms of saved money. Luckily, the chances of you feeling a 2-degree difference is slim, so your comfort will remain well intact. There are some people who have gone as far as 5-degrees, which would save you more money, but you would also definitely suffer noticeably. Like I said earlier, as people save more and more money, more of these things seem tolerable in the name of seeing that bank account grow, but I believe a two-degree change is more than enough to get started. Some modern thermostats allow you to set timers as well, which will change the temperature by 7 or 8 degrees while you are at work most of the day and will have your home back to a comfortable level in time for you to walk through the door. This works great if everyone is on a similar daily schedule, but again, this phase is all about doing what you can and are willing to, not forcing yourself to suffer for a few extra dollars.

Now that you have made lifestyle changes (and I hope you took some notes or highlighted or something because there's a lot of information to act on), you can start adding money into that new bank account of yours each month and watch that number grow. Once you've got enough in there to start making some purchases, then phase 2 goes into effect. Congratulations, you are officially making more money off your home, without spending 1$, you're helping to stall climate change, and you're ready to start doing some real damage to that electric bill.

Chapter 5: Phase 2- Let's Start Investing

You have a separate bank account set up, and you've been depositing the money you're saving every single month, so you know the exact dollar amount you've got to work with. Everybody does phase 1 differently, so everyone will have a different amount put away, but when you get up around 100$ in that account, it is time to start spending what you've made back on some efficient technologies. This is the phase in which those behaviors you've taken on and fostered start turning your home into a building that is LITERALLY worth more on the market than it was because it is more energy-efficient. We're going to start with lighting and move up to the ventilation of your home, and heating/cooling envelope (I told you they would be back).

The first change I always suggest to people looking to invest in efficiency is to replace all incandescent bulbs with LED lights instead. It is easy in terms of installation (changing a light bulb) and is in my opinion the most inexpensive start to this phase. It only costs a few dollars per bulb to make the upgrade, so you can get through this step quickly which is nice. LED light bulbs also last approximately 2000% longer than standard incandescent bulbs and 400% longer than a CFL bulb, so they are pricier at first look, but you hardly ever need to replace them. For each bulb that you switch from incandescent to LED, you can save between 5$ and 10$ per year. Extrapolate this out to 20-25 bulbs changed out, and you are looking at 75$ per year to 200$ per year depending on how often the bulbs are in use. Even switching just the 5 most used lights in your home (kitchen, living room, hallways) you can save about 40$ in the year. Obviously, making this switch pays for itself quickly, which is the goal behind each of the purchases suggested in phase 2. When you add these savings on top of your still happening phase 1 savings, you're looking at making an additional 200-400 a year and we still haven't even made an actual investment into your homes water or HVAC systems.

So, in your first year of phase 2, we've gotten you up to about 200$ per year that you didn't have previously. As I have said, this isn't a get rich quick sort of thing, but an elaborate plan that takes years to work through and pays out at the end if you have the discipline. I'll follow that sentiment up with the mention of storm windows.

One of the most underrated and unknown facts of heat loss is how much escapes/enters through your windows each year. If you have a home like mine (giant windows directly in the front of the home) and don't know this, the amount of energy lost through those window panes will be inexorable. Luckily, converting to storm windows is an effective way to combat this loss. This is the first step towards really combatting your energy bill, and it comes to the tune of up to 400$ per year. If you have single-paned windows and throw storm windows over them, that 400$ is about the number you'll see. That's IN ADDITION TO the 300$ or so you've made from making the other changes and investments so far. Now, if you have double-paned windows already (which are great themselves) adding a storm layer on will save you about 100$ per year. It is not as drastic but considering that this is being paid for out of the money that you've made through investments already put into your home, it doesn't matter so much. To put a storm window in place is going to cost you about 100$ per window (if you can find less than that, jump all over it) so using your savings can get you 2 or 3 windows done in your first year. Then another 3 or 4 the next and so on and so forth. The more windows you get done, the more you'll save and the more you can do the next year. That is the compounding of savings into money you're making that has come up time and time again througnout this book.

We are halfway through phase 2, and you've increased the amount of money you will be putting away each year to at the absolute minimum 500$. In most cases, it will be a number much greater than this, but even with only 500$, you can start making investments that will drop your bill even further. These will come in the form of insulation improvements (heating and cooling AGAIN).

Your insulation has more to do with your energy bill that the electronics and lighting realistically ever could. Insulation is also surprisingly inexpensive to install (although when it's all extra money the cost doesn't matter). There are the little improvements that you can make first for a VERY small amount of money. These include putting sealant strips on your doors, throwing curtains up over your windows (it is the clear surfaces that really kill us) and consistently checking for leaks and cracks in your frames. Once the little things have been handled, it is time to insulate the crap out of ANYWHERE that you can. Easily installed insulation such as glass fiber, cellulose or pre-cut drywall are all readily available and inexpensive. This improves your home envelope (the casing around your home that keeps heat inside in the summer and outside in the winter) drastically, and obviously brings your energy bill down with it. Insulation improvements done by a professional can run you over 1000$, but you can buy a roll of insulation and do it yourself for a few hundred. Making improvements to your insulation can save you about 400$ a year though, so even if you go the most expensive route, the insulation will pay for itself in only 3 years' time.

You should also certainly wrap your water and gas heater with insulation. So many people do not insulate their water heater, even though it can cut hot water costs by nearly 50%. In doing this, you should also insulate the pipes that carry your hot water and the heat produced from your gas burner/furnace/heat pump. In terms of cost-effective insulation for your home, getting the water heater, gas heater, and respective pipes done is one of the cheapest ways to yield great results. The reason I put this after and separate from the general insulation section however is because of phase 3. There is a high chance the time will come that you will have enough money saved to purchase new high-efficiency gas and water heating systems. It is because of this that, even though in the right now it is a great way to save some money, it may be in your best interests to hold off if purchasing a heat pump or new water heater is something you foresee yourself doing. It is entirely up to you which route to take, I just want to make sure you have all the information at your disposal, so you can make solid, well- educated investment decisions.

Phase 2 is the one in which the big dents in your bill start to come to fruition. Ideally, you are saving at least 750$ per year by the end, and with that much extra income, making bigger purchases with only saved money will start to look possible. Whether you want to stop here or follow through all the way to solar panels (if your home fits the qualifications) is up to you, but it is in phase 3 that the big investments that can take your home to that true net-zero energy level will come into play.

Chapter 6: Phase 3- The Big Stuff

This is it folks. The phase where the most expensive investments will be made, and your homes will see the biggest investment to savings value. There are only a few more investments to go if you've decided to take it to this level, and I couldn't be happier that I've inspired you to act and start bringing your electric bill down.

It is in this phase that your patience and discipline will most be called upon the most. With the other 2 phases, immediate changes produced immediate results, and the savings to investment back to savings turnover hopefully happened quickly. At this phase, you are hopefully saving that 750-1000 mark each year, and as such can afford to buy energy-efficient appliances. The issue is that energy-efficient appliances are significantly more expensive than insulation or windows. It could take 1-3 years just to save enough money to get one appliance. I know it's hard to see that money grow, and with the stresses of day to day life, not touch it, but if you can hold out, you can see serious fiduciary benefits begin to unfold.

Your stove, refrigerator, dishwasher, washing machine, dryer, water tank, and gas heater, are all the things I'm referring to when discussing "The Big Stuff". Using the refrigerator as an example, buying an energy star approved refrigerator costs about 1000-1500. Those dollars are your entire years' savings and then some! But, this one appliance will save you around 300$ a year on your electric bill. Now your yearly savings have reached at least 1000$, so the next appliance you get can be afforded in a shorter time span. You purchase the next one, again for around the same amount of money, and your savings compound and grow even further. I trust you can research the exact amount it will cost/save you to buy each appliance and decide what you are and aren't willing to do based on your own time frame.

At this phase, it is up to you to use your money the best way you know how, and with the varying range in cost of these appliances and the differing needs of your families, I couldn't possibly say what it will cost/save you with accuracy. What I can say is that energy-efficient appliances use about 50% of the standard. With that in mind, you can expect your bill to go down 50% if you complete the turnover of every appliance I mentioned at the beginning of this chapter. If you were saving 1000$ a year at the end of phase 2, you can expect to be saving 1500$ a year by the end of this part of phase 3. It is with this money that you will purchase your panels.

A typical electric bill in the United States costs families about 2000$ a year. If you are down to 500$ per year, using the broad numbers I mentioned before, that means you only need a solar system that can cover that amount rather than the 2000$ a month you would've needed previously. An average American home uses approximately 920 kWh per month, so we can accompany this value with the 2000$ a year mark for argument's sake. If you need to cover (again these are all averages and every situation is different) one quarter of the 920 kWh mark, since your electric bill is down to about one quarter of what it was, you only need to get a solar system that will produce 250 kWh per month (and this would be a system projected to overproduce). This means, in the most simplistic case, you would require less than a 1 kW solar system if you were to divide the number of kWh your home uses in a month by the number of hours that there are in a month.

Now, my math here was incredibly basic as again I couldn't possibly understand your situation; but in theory, if you used my plan to its fullest potential, the cost of adding solar panels into your home will be a fraction of what it was. In the year 2018, solar energy costs a little over 3$ per watt, so installing a 1 kW system costs a little more than 3000$. That is only three years' worth of saving for you, and suddenly your energy bill has gone below zero, you haven't spent one meaningful dollar, and you've put a system that should overproduce electricity into your home.

Your net zero energy home is now a hot commodity. With the push towards a greener earth and living, there are tax breaks and incentives you wouldn't believe that are available for people working towards net zero energy homes. Some states offer straight up cash bonuses for EVERY SINGLE energy efficient appliance you install. Others, as mentioned earlier, will pay you out for any electricity you overproduce using your newly installed (and owned) solar panels. Now you are truly making more money off your home, and it didn't cost you one dollar to get started and build your home into something more financially useful to you, and good for the environment as well.

Chapter 7: What It's All Worth

In the last few chapters, I have given you some knowledge about bringing down your electric bill. I am sure you could've just googled any of the things I presented to you, and I genuinely hope that you DO google these things and acquire as much information as possible about the topic. How to bring down your energy bill isn't the lesson I've tried to instill in you all throughout this book. It is merely an example of what a disciplined and informed financial mindset can bring about.

Using the financial techniques I've put forward; you have turned your home into something you will own sooner, pay less for over time, and can sell at a higher price when that time comes. It didn't happen overnight. You had to put the effort forth and make it happen. Once you decided to act, the savings started snowballing and in the timespan over which you were projected to own your home anyway, you've increased its value substantially.

What will you do with the money now? Continue to put it into a separate account and let it grow into more? Maybe, you can save up for a new car, or another home. You can put that money towards your children's college education, or in a whole-life life insurance policy (if you do not know what this is, look into it IMMEDIATELY as it is one of the best investments you can make in your future if you get the information early enough). All I'm saying is, don't stop here.

What you've learned is an infinitely valuable skill, that can be used to build true long-term wealth for the rest of your life. Do little things to save money, track those savings, and spend the money accordingly. Whether you want to go on a vacation, or start a business, make sure you know WHERE the money you're using for those endeavors is coming from. Take the example of energy-efficiency and use it across any facet of your life you see fit.

I am offering my own excel spreadsheet template for tracking your energy savings to those who follow my Facebook page at Randy Kent and send me a message with your name and e-mail address. This is where I'll post new information I acquire and any revolutions in the field that I come across. If you have ANY questions about your personal energy situation, let me know and we can work together to get you started on your path to a sustainable life and financial freedom. I would greatly appreciate if you guys could give me reviews on Amazon, so I know how to improve my writing and help you out more the next time around.

Happy Saving,

Randy J. Kent

www.ingramcontent.com/pod-product-compliance
Lightning Source LLC
Chambersburg PA
CBHW030513220526
45464CB00006B/2772